GLORIOUS TENSION

GLORIOUS TENSION

Rediscovering Our
SACRED MIDDLE GROUND
in an Age of Extremism

PAUL W. HOBBY

PROPAGANDA
PRESENTS, INC

GLORIOUS TENSION

Rediscovering Our Sacred Middle Ground in an Age of Extremism

FIRST EDITION

ISBN 978-1-5445-4152-5 *Hardcover*
      978-1-5445-4151-8 *Paperback*
      978-1-5445-4150-1 *Ebook*

For Janet, Grace, Walker, and Eric, with love everlasting...

Contents

Courage is the midpoint between two vices—cowardice being the best known, but recklessness being equally dangerous.

—TEACHINGS OF ARISTOTLE

Initial Self-Diagnostic

If you have been as critical of your "side" as you have been of the other "side," then you don't need to read this. If you haven't called balls and strikes objectively, you do need to read this. If you knew exactly who the other side was when you read the first sentence, you really need to read this, because they are controlling your behavior. That's never good. If you tend to defend your side by attacking the other side, consider that you might be part of the problem.

Introduction

Years from now, cultural anthropologists will look at our times and notice what they don't see. Our traditional respect for reason and compromise has gone missing. American unity sounds more like a dark-money political action committee than a current reality. Petty differences in neighborhood associations and school boards have become an excuse to launch seething nuclear rhetoric.

On that topic, you and I are probably drawn into the same basic conversations over and over again. At church. At work. At school. At dinner gatherings. Why is America so polarized? Why are people so hostile? Why can't people get along the way they used to?

I'll tell you why: the middle has lost its agency, its franchise, and its place of honor. The center is no longer legitimate or safe. We have lost respect for compromise and the tools that support it. In a hashtag world, people conflate balance with mental and moral weakness. *If you are for boys, you are against girls. If you acknowledge the physical realities that created women's sports, you are transphobic. If you are pro-choice, you are anti-life.*

These false binaries represent toxic nonsense and lazy internet prattle. Recall that legislative bodies are purposefully co-located so members can confer and reason together, but now the floor mic is just another stage for performance art to stoke a rabid political base. One senator I know describes modern Washington simply as "shirts and skins." For all the good things electronic communication has done for us, it has decimated the processes that discover peaceful consensus. "Wedge issues" have lived up to their name. Scorched-earth, strident secularism, and vicious behaviors are now more the rule than the exception in public discourse.

I offer this collection of essays to provide evidence that the premise of coexistence is compromise. The glorious tension between conflicting ideas has gotten us this far, and abandoning the virtues of compromise seems perilous. My intention is to provide an argument for rehabilitating the middle—more accurately, for rehabilitating those who have lost their taste for the middle, in favor of the sugar-high of extremism. As I will explain, the unfortunate truth is human brains easily succumb to addiction to our own closed loop.

As we perform a flyover of the mental terrain generally known as the middle, I beseech you to search your own rhetoric and belief system. Stop defending, and start relating. You might discover that common ground is sacred ground. It had better be, because it is nothing less than the guardian of peace and prosperity. Be assured that it doesn't tend itself. Consider the ancient storying recounting the tragedy of the commons: as British economist

William Forster Lloyd noted, without any sense of ownership, people take resources like public pastures for granted. They act in their own short-term self-interest, spoiling the shared space for everyone—including, eventually, themselves.

Make no mistake: the shared resource system at stake for us is the middle ground—the place consensus, and therefore liberty, lives.

Before the final essay's call to action, I hope you will, at a minimum, feel more familiar with the middle. Perhaps you might recognize it more vividly in your surroundings, and maybe even celebrate its genius and learn how to find it and defend it with vigor. Ultimately, you may even agree that while ideology helps to frame an issue, it rarely helps resolve one. The real work starts where ideology ends, through factual investigation, impartial reasoning, and listening to other people. Not only does compromise keep the peace; it also tends to provide a better answer on the merits. As quoted in Walter Isaacson's book *Benjamin Franklin: An American Life*, Benjamin Franklin said, "Compromisers may not make great heroes, but they do make great democracies," and, "For him, compromise was not only a practical approach but a moral one. Tolerance, humility, and a respect for others required it."

The center deserves center stage right now. As I write this, Vladimir Putin is killing innocent Ukrainians with impunity because the middle cannot exist in Russia. Vocal opposition is quite literally illegal—moderation and consensus are not part of Putin's plan, and they never have been (sham elections notwithstanding). Friction and debate provide the forge of consensus, but autocrats don't tolerate those activities.

So the stakes are high. People who don't scare easily are scared of what our future may hold. I am one of them. I wrote most of these essays before the events of January 6, 2021, a day that provided an unwelcome confirmation of all my foreboding sentiment.

My ultimate goal is to foster a feeling of your ownership of the middle while suggesting a tool kit with which to defend it. That outcome requires a continuous internal vigilance and a willingness to use your voice, even—or especially—when it's uncomfortable.

Martin Luther King Jr. famously said, "In the end we will remember not the words of our enemies but the silence of our friends." By the time you finish reading, that sentence may reso-nate in ways you hadn't considered. At some point, confronting your friends is part of defending the middle. Silence is easy when your friends are wrong. Our mirrors hold both the problem and the solution.

CHAPTER ONE

What Is at Stake?

Cultivated mind is the guardian genius of democracy...It is the only dictator that freemen acknowledge and the only security that freemen desire.

—MIRABEAU B. LAMAR, PRESIDENT
OF THE REPUBLIC OF TEXAS

In 1935, as fascism grew in Europe, Sinclair Lewis published a semi-satirical novel titled *It Can't Happen Here.* It describes the rise of Berzelius "Buzz" Windrip, who critics at the time viewed as a proxy for Huey Long. Buzz defeats Franklin Delano Roosevelt and is elected president of the United States using the time-honored tyrant's tool kit: foment fear of aliens and promise drastic economic and social reforms as part of a nationalistic return to patriotism and "traditional" values. After his election, Windrip ignores the foundational institutions of American government while mustering a ruthless paramilitary force.

In March 1937, Colonel Oveta Culp Hobby, who was the founder of the Women's Army Corps as well as my grandmother, gave an address to a national women's group that provided a provocative counterpoint to Mr. Lewis's book. Her speech achieved a measure of fame and was reprinted in a number of newspapers nationally. I reproduce here the essence of her remarks just as the attentive world was beginning to understand what Adolf Hitler really was:

"What can happen here?" you ask.

I answer, "Liberty can be strangled or stifled here in the United States—vaunted fortress of freedom." Sinclair Lewis took a negative premise and unfolded its paradox. I take a positive premise and reveal its legitimacy.

How does it happen that talk of dictators can be countenanced in the United States? Or call a rose by any other name—

This nation came into being because men had become a law unto nations. This country was settled, wrested from a crown, and conceived in democracy because the men who came here preferred a nation that was subservient to the rights and wishes of men rather than a country composed of a group of serfs who were vassals of a king.

How short our memories grow! It has happened over and over again the world over. Italy still thrills to the name of Garibaldi thinking of him as the founder of a strong nation. They have forgotten that his heroic struggle had the single purpose of freedom. Had they remembered, the iron jaw would not be superimposed on the map of Italy. Russian peasants tiring of their centuries of starvation and cruelty, threw off the yoke of the Czars. They took hope and marched forward until Stalin again hitched them to a yoke of tyranny red with the blood of political opposition.

From the far corners of the earth, the musicians, writers and scientists of Germany hid wet eyes when they hear "Deutschland über Alles." Those who loved liberty under Von Hindenburg are long since dead. An Austrian house painter painted a glowing picture for a discouraged and humiliated Germany. His landscape glows with concentration camps, bruised bodies, and tortured spirits. He has taught his people to love hate. The swastika is the flag; Heil Hitler is the national anthem; and the salute their attitude of worship. German women bear children as a command performance. Their cultural progress has been halted. Their children will make excellent cannon fodder in Hitler's attempt to prove that the culture and spirit of Germany is not dead—just their sons!

Spain...glamorous country of the Alhambra, engages in wholesale murder to prove that each contestant possesses superior qualifications to govern. That they both possess superior qualifications to extinguish a race and ravage the beauty and antiquity of Spain admits of no doubt.

Greece, home of the world's oldest democracy, does a goose step under a monarchial baron.

At what time in the gradual disintegration that these countries have experienced, do you suppose the people organized themselves as vigilantes and questioned every act of the state? Do you suppose they applied the test of freedom to every new power the government exercised, or did they, as so many of us, say, "It can't happen here!"

If one could see the army of the dictator or hear the clink of his armored heel, resistance would be everywhere evident, but dictators of the twentieth century vintage are commanding orators, makers of fine phrase, zealots for the rights of the citizens, descendants of Moses who have been sent to lead us from the Wilderness.

Dictators are not heaven-sent but hell-born, and the borning is neither obvious nor immediate.

If I proved that it can happen here, and I think I have, your next question is "How can it happen here?"

My answer is: "We are indifferent to our heritage. Familiarity has bred contempt. The liberty we have known so well has become a prophet without honor in his own country. We are indicted on the charge of indifference."

Rights and privileges which we accept as a matter of course were handed us because our forebears refused to sacrifice liberty, wherever, whenever, however the demands were made. The road to freedom was wet with the blood of braver men and women than we.

Indifference, the least thoughtful of us know, is the most potent tool of the despot. Indolence is the subsoil in which the seeds of dictatorship fall and germinate. Willing ignorance is the precursor of an enslaved people...Let us, you and I, examine the origin of our liberty and renew our acquaintance with its growth.

The first great document of human liberty is the Magna Carta...

With the signing of this instrument a new dawn of freedom broke upon a world black with tyranny. There at Runnymede alongside the River Thames in 1215, King John did promise that he would no more "send upon, imprison, nor disseize any man or deprive him of life and liberty except by the judgment of his peers and the law of land." Thus a people who had thrown off indifference forced a ruler mad with power to sign the great document of human rights, the Magna Carta. Government by law attained legal status for the first time. Freedom began her long weary climb to constitutional government and a division of the powers of the government with the signing of this instrument...

The next great document in the evolution of liberty is the English Bill of Rights. It was written as a revolutionary measure after James was deposed. When William and Mary came to the throne, they accepted the provisions laid down in the Bill of Rights. It was afterward introduced and passed by the Parliament. It embodied the fundamental principles of human and political liberties. As you know, the first ten amendments to the Federal Constitution form the American Bill of Rights. Many state constitutions have Bill of Rights.

The eighteenth century saw the fundamental fight for liberty removed from England to the Americas. The men and women who came to colonize America brought with them a passionate devotion to the principles of freedom which their forefathers had tried to establish in England. Englishmen had become indifferent and the liberties of Englishmen were again flouted.

Those who loved liberty came to America because conditions at home were intolerable. They hoped that here in America they might enjoy the freedom that obtains where there is no tyranny.

For a while the colonists enjoyed their much-prized freedom. Soon *however, tyranny began its encroachments. The American Declaration of Independence was the answer. It is perhaps the most powerful indictment of tyranny ever voiced by free men.*

In language that defies time and change, it is stated that the freedom of man is an inherent right. No words more significant to mankind were ever penned than these:

"We hold these truths to be self-evident, that all men are created equal, that they are endowed by their creator with certain inalienable rights; that among these are life, liberty, and the pursuit of happiness; that to secure these rights, governments are instituted among men, deriving their just powers from the consent of the governed; that whenever any form of government becomes destructive of these ends, it is the right of the people to alter or to abolish it, and to institute new government, laying its foundation on such principles and organizing its powers in such form, as to them shall seem most likely to affect their safety and happiness."

In 1779, Thomas Jefferson presented to the Virginia Legislature a bill "for the more general diffusion of knowledge," a measure which recognized for the first time in America, the principle that education is a function of the government.

Slowly his theories were accepted. The Texas Declaration of Independence, adopted March 2, 1836, a little more than a century ago declared, "It is an axiom of political science, that unless a people are educated and enlightened, it is idle to expect the continuance of civil liberty, or the capacity for self-government."

A beacon light for American liberty now and forever is Washington's refusal to become King. After the revolution, there are many Amer-

icans who favored an elective monarchy based upon the British system. General Washington was strongly urged to make himself king of an American Empire.

Washington wrote, "Be assured, sir, no occurrence in the course of the war has given me more painful sensations than your information of there being such ideas existing in the Army as you have expressed and I must view with abhorrence, and reprehend with severity...I am much at a loss to conceive what part of my conduct could have given encouragement to an address which to me seems big with the greatest mischiefs that can befall my Country...Let me conjure you then, if you have any regard for your Country...concern for yourself, or posterity, or respect for me to banish these thoughts from your mind, and never communicate as from yourself, or anyone else, a sentiment of like nature."

Thus, one great American statesman refused a concentration of power knowing full well as do all students of government what the inevitable outcome is.

The constitution sets up a triple division of powers of the government. The executive is one branch, the legislative is another, and the judicial is another. Every great document I have recounted was promulgated in an effort to divide the powers of government. Our knowledge of human nature should tell us that power in the hands of one person ultimately means the abuse of that power...

Listen with open minds to both sides of a question. Let your rational judgment rather than your emotional judgment control. Once your mind is made up that a measure will endanger the wealth of liberty you hold in trusteeship, oppose it with all the strength and ingenuity at your command.

In closing, I quote John Stuart Mill:

"A people may prefer a free government; but, if from indolence or carelessness or cowardice or want of public spirit, they are unequal to the exertions necessary for preserving it; if they will not fight for it when directly attacked; if they can be deluded by the artifices used to cheat them out of it; if by momentary discouragement or temporary panic, or a fit of enthusiasm for an individual, they can be induced to lay their liberties at the feet of even a great man, or trust him with powers which enable him to subvert their institutions—in all these cases they are more or less unfit for liberty."

During the next year, we shall know whether or not Americans are fit for liberty!

The "next year" she spoke of was 1939, and as the world knows now, Americans were in fact "fit for liberty"—ours and everyone else's, as it turned out. That Greatest Generation surely groaned in their graves eighty-two years later when domestic totalitarianism attempted to seize its moment. The very thing Colonel Hobby had warned of had come to pass.

As we know, an armed insurrection—by a violent mob attempting to preserve a despot whom democracy had rejected—did happen here on January 6, 2021. This event was not issue-based civil disobedience like the Boston Tea Party, Shays' Rebellion, the Whiskey Rebellion, the raid on Harpers Ferry, or the civil rights march on the Edmund Pettus Bridge. What we saw on January 6 was an attack on the ultimate issue of democracy itself—at the very cathedral of its global identity. If you thought those events were negligible or anything other than a stain on our history, this book might not be a good use of your time.

CHAPTER TWO

What the Middle Is and Is Not

Literalism is for the weak; fundamentalism is for the insecure. Both are sins, too...for to come to believe that we are in exclusive possession of the truth about things beyond time and space...is to put ourselves in the place of God.

—JON MEACHAM, *THE HOPE OF GLORY*

The very word *freedom* is too often used to mean freedom from the social contract that created the greatest nation in the history of the world. Humor is hazardous. *Weaponized* is a ubiquitous new term, applied in almost any context imaginable. As a result, the once vital center has become paralyzed. On a growing list of subjects, what once was a bell curve of public opinion now looks more like a barbell.

Why else would Arthur Brooks, keynote speaker at the 68th annual National Prayer Breakfast call our country to action with a cry for biblical love? He believes "the biggest crisis facing our nation and many other nations today...[is] the crisis of contempt and polarization that's tearing our societies apart."

It is not a coincidence that as more and more subjects have become political rather than scientific, and as fewer subjects remain legitimate topics of rational discussion, both parties have systemically eliminated the center of political debate. Some thoughtful voices see haunting parallels between pre-Bolshevik Russia and America today. The basic elements supporting that observation are a disaffected political nationalism and a wide disparity of wealth, both coincident with an arrogant, dismissive movement within academia and media to condemn history, dethrone historical figures, and delegitimatize capitalism and religion. The old cliché that our free-market system turns everything into dollars, while communism turns everything into politics feels less true all the time. Dollars are passé when the United States government is $31 trillion in debt. Cryptocurrency gains legitimacy as a result of our poor stewardship of the world's reserve currency. Balanced budgets and limited resources frame compromise, whereas politics frame division and false choices.

Weary guardians of the sunny, transcendent patriotism that has characterized the American identity for centuries are all asking some version of the same questions: Where did the middle go? How did the middle ground in our politics and society become so uninhabitable? Did it divide evenly into warring camps? Has it been expunged by political correctness run amok? Did it become overly entitled or radicalized by social media? Did it go underground, or is it actually extinct? It's because of gerrymandering, right? Or legalized cannabis—yeah, that's it; didn't I tell you so?

In these essays, we will consider root causes, but history isn't the object of this exercise. Forensics are less important than future behaviors. How much should we care? Haven't factions in society seemed this irreconcilable before? Is this time really that different? I believe the answer is yes—that we are experiencing an odd flattening of the social bell curve that makes the middle harder to find. To find it, we need to define it, explain why it is important, and understand where it comes from.

We need to consider the basic chemistry of compromise. That is how conflict normally gets resolved—or doesn't. In my experience, so long as the parties can define a shared objective and agree on a set of facts, the middle will prevail without bloodshed, whether in business or politics.

But there is no shared objective (much less agreed-upon facts) in many conversations today, scientific or otherwise. That is why the gender card, or the race card, or the class-warfare card is now the first played in any public dispute, an easy move regardless of specific underlying facts. Canned responses place the other side in an irreconcilable "you haven't lived it, so you can't ever get it" position, forever consigning its members to opposition across the cultural abyss. In truth, that separation is often the only real objective. When the opposing parties thrive on perpetuating their own angry victim complexes, agreement isn't the prize; it is a price neither is willing to pay.

In a pre-COVID world, some fantasized that a crisis might bring us together. The reality was far different. COVID has been an accelerant, driving herd behaviors toward some future we don't recognize. Moderates wander lost, looking for a friend across a wasteland of invective. That friend has to be you and me because, as we will see, extremism is about false choices, straw men, and other word games that can escalate into direr consequences.

We got a taste of those consequences for a day in early 2021. Like many others, I was sick to my stomach watching Americans, claiming to be patriots, erecting gallows on the Capitol grounds and parading Confederate flags though the building on January 6. I felt even sicker to see elected officials make light of the riot despite the obvious gravity of the brutal videos.

Karl Rove delivers an entertaining and well-informed riff on the Gilded Age, arguing persuasively that America of the late nineteenth century was much more divided than it is now. I appreciate his command of history and sincerely hope he's right that the system will resolve itself in due time. But my anxiety remains because gladiator politics and winner-take-all contests portend big mistakes. The notions of balance and "reasoning together" are essential, as the spoils of extremist victory are dangerous—politically dangerous when public officials muzzle their opponents with dark money, and physically dangerous when domestic terrorists try to prevent a peaceful transfer of power.

Consider some examples of structurally juxtaposed ideas:

- consistency and change
- grace and truth
- communism and capitalism
- individual responsibility and group identity
- yin and yang
- luck and hard work
- the double helix
- sun and rain

- carrots and sticks
- nature and nurture

What these pairings have in common is that none pose binary choices in application. Opposing ideas are not incompatible. In fact, each pairing is fundamentally interdependent.

How many times has a journalist or historian has ended up at the cliché "as it turns out, the truth is somewhere in between"? Biographers weigh the views of those who see their subject as a "tyrant" or a "visionary" and rarely end up at either end of that spectrum. Astronomers who ponder quantum physics and the origins of the universe rarely reject opposing theories as much as they find a way to meld them. *Both*—in some balance—is almost always the right answer.

The center is an alloy, forged by the extremes it defies. In thermodynamics, a critical state is where a substance is two things at once. There is an interesting word for that phenomenon in chemistry and in the English language: *antimony* is both a periodic element and an important idea. As an element, antimony possesses physical and chemical properties that fall between the metal and nonmetal categories, making it neither a conductor nor an insulator. It is toxic unless alloyed with another element and for that reason is sometimes referred to as the "loneliest element."

The literary side of the word, which has a subtly different spelling but common linguistic heritage, is related in meaning: *antinomy* describes an irreconcilable dilemma between one law or principle and another or a philosophical contradiction between two statements despite their both seeming to have a basis in sound reasoning. Either side would be incorrect (and therefore logically fatal) without the other.

Democracy rests on antinomy, as does free-market capitalism. Inherent in both systems are the inputs of millions of individual decisions. Elections and markets continually and relentlessly redefine the middle. But even as we revere democratic processes and the efficiencies of free markets, both systems come with important caveats. For example, our federal constitution prescribes one coequal branch to be led by nine unelected justices with lifetime appointments who are chosen by an officeholder not elected by popular vote. One can hardly imagine a less democratic idea. The point is that the judicial branch occurs in a context that does have more accountable features—there is a glorious balance in the larger construct of the Constitution. In commerce, no one seriously advocates a market completely free from government regulation. Air traffic control, food safety, orderly financial markets, and basic consumer protection all justify a role for government that can affect markets. Markets not only tolerate but require the balance of a public sector that prevents exploitive behaviors by irresponsible market actors. Thus, sweeping ideological statements and sanctimonious arm-waving are of little value in these realms.

Without measured language, shared culture, sober leadership, and trusted institutions to help us accomplish consensus at the middle, less peaceful means will prevail.

It is an article of faith in progressive thought that racial or religious "intolerance" is evil, the Holocaust being the most vivid example of intolerance in horrific action. Many on the right, however, see the tolerance movement as an undue restraint on free speech, particularly on college campuses. Who is correct? They both are. If we generalize language to associate mass murder with any idea we find disagreeable, we make *tolerance* a term not of inclusion, but of censorship.

Similarly, the idea that our society is "stronger through diversity" should strengthen the middle. But that idea has been hijacked to lionize an identity politics in which each group is hypersensitized to offense by all the others. Like tolerance, it becomes the cudgel of political correctness—where tension gives way to taboo and the advocates of greater diversity become intolerant of opposing views.

Consider a recent case in which a University of Virginia college student stood up and said, without a hint of irony or self-awareness, "This is the MSC [multicultural student center], and frankly there's just too many white people in here, and this is a space for people of color." Multicultural becomes code for exclusion rather than diversity. Notice the pattern: when even moderate ideas like tolerance and diversity turn into dogmatic mantras, they become destructively exclusionist.

Oversimplification is a siren song to the lazy. In the social media realm, "calling out" is when you over-simplify the other person's argument, and "trolling" is when it happens to you. The ten-dollar verb for one version of oversimplification is "to conflate," meaning to associate distinct ideas for persuasive purposes.

That tactic is the reserve currency of political consultants and other manipulators across time—because it often succeeds. Enough dollars invested in a false narrative can make it seem true. Practitioners find out quickly that no one calls balls and strikes in the intellectual honesty game. When pressed or shamed, they respond predictably: "The other side is behaving even worse, so we are just responding in kind because we are forced to." As a result, the race to the bottom never ends.

Sloppy logic is dangerous. Facts matter. Words have meaning. Circumstances require discernment, not binary choices. So is tolerance a good thing or not? What about diversity? *To a point* is the answer.

Get used to that answer...

Einstein would have failed as a political consultant, given that he's frequently paraphrased as saying, "Everything should be made as simple as possible, but not simpler." If he needed to ponder cosmic questions on a case-by-case basis, you and I should probably not behave any differently.

There is another spring trap in current rhetorical practice that we need to acknowledge. Any appeal to a middle way in public debate today risks immediate interpretation as an endorsement of the listener's opponent. This little move allows the responder to "get back to their talking points" rather than addressing a question about their own position. All questions about Trump trigger answers about Pelosi (or Clinton or Obama), and the reverse is also true. Rhetorical deflection is not new, but in this polarized landscape, it's now reflexive and accepted behavior. In fact, cable news designs coverage around the idea that the best defense is a counterstrike. Jerry Springer showed the way.

Rather than taking the bait to derail the conversation, intellectually honest people often decide not to engage. Reason gets smothered in its crib. The new rules dictate that there are victims, so there must be villains—creating scar tissue rather than solutions. People learn avoidance of moderation and its complexities as a rhetorical tactic, but defending and cultivating the middle is not a word game. It is an exercise in humility, mutual respect, and hard choices.

Certainty too often precedes hatred. The toxicity of hatred in practice is on display every day in our news feed, with the Middle East often providing lessons about the results of hatred spawned by religious certainty.

I am not an end-times prophecy kind of guy, but I am paying attention. As I write this, an imperialist Russian dictator is invading Ukraine and a militaristic China clearly intends to terminate any civil liberties for the Taiwanese. Neither electoral math nor science matters to a party of one. Things do fall apart.

One of William Butler Yeats's most influential poems is "The Second Coming," and it's of particular relevance to the notion of centrism:

> Turning and turning in the widening gyre
> The falcon cannot hear the falconer;
> Things fall apart; the centre cannot hold;
> Mere anarchy is loosed upon the world,
> The blood-dimmed tide is loosed, and everywhere
> The ceremony of innocence is drowned;
> The best lack all conviction, while the worst
> Are full of passionate intensity.

> Surely some revelation is at hand;

Surely the Second Coming is at hand.
The Second Coming! Hardly are those words out
When a vast image out of *Spiritus Mundi*
Troubles my sight: somewhere in sands of the desert
A shape with lion body and the head of a man,
A gaze blank and pitiless as the sun,
Is moving its slow thighs, while all about it
Reel shadows of the indignant desert birds.
The darkness drops again; but now I know
That twenty centuries of stony sleep
Were vexed to nightmare by a rocking cradle,
And what rough beast, its hour come round at last,
Slouches towards Bethlehem to be born?

Do we live in the time when "the centre cannot hold," when "mere anarchy is loosed upon the world" and the "best lack all conviction"? And if the "worst are full of passionate intensity," how will we know which is which? I, too, wonder "what rough beast...slouches towards Bethlehem to be born"—has "its hour come round at last"?

Yeats's haunting words can be read as a dour prophecy, and such predictions seldom play out. Most often, the messy middle perseveres, making incremental progress toward longer lives, lower rates of poverty, expanded access to education, social justice, and so on. But that progress is in peril when we forget how to fight fair. In a way that Yeats's dark dream foreshadowed, "the ceremony of innocence is drowned."

I'm reminded of the famous Goya etching in which menacing ravens circle a prostrate figure, *El sueño de la razón produce monstruos* (*The Sleep of Reason Produces Monsters*). As famed biographer Jon Meacham writes in his Christian homily, *The Hope of Glory*, "For all its limitations, reason—the weighing of evidence, the assessment of likelihood, the capacity to shift one's opinions in light of thought and of experience—remains essential."

Community requires a few common elements: shared fear, shared greed, and shared virtue. And if the third part isn't present, the first two don't work very well together. Extremism drives a very narrow sense of community in which sharing itself is suspect and believers cherish their absolute knowledge of the truth. Such isolation and certitude present an obstacle when it comes to problem-solving or peacemaking.

Those who remain silent, not out of fear but disgust and help-lessness, hollow out whatever remains of our moderate core. I do not exempt myself from that criticism. We watch the waves of populism breaking from the right and then the left with a purposeful remove. Culture wars and identity politics baffle us for their feral nature. Shouting voices seem to reject all we thought that our experiment in multicultural democracy had taught the world. Do "the best lack all conviction," as Yeats suspected we would?

Any number of organizations have formed to organize the middle, but none has yet catalyzed the faithful in any powerful way. To be fair, their task is difficult. Modern centrists don't fill many stadiums or appear on many cable channels. The story of the three bears' porridge may be as close to a star turn as the middle ever had.

On the new website Denison Forum, Claire Avidon correctly

suggests that the very concept of civility now paints images of weakness rather than respect. She notes that in an interview with *New York Times* journalist Nellie Bowles, Professor James Calvin Davis of Middlebury College, author of *In Defense of Civility*, stated, "There isn't even agreement anymore on whether civility is a good thing."

In addition to taking a patronizing stance toward civility, there are certain strange moments when extremists stop shooting at each other and instead target moderation itself. They are bombing the bridge, and that is preface to something even darker than January 6. The dynamic reminds me of a fateful conversation, recounted in Frederic Morton's *Thunder at Twilight: Vienna 1913–1914*:

> "The Archduke has a special weapon. He will use it if we let him come to power. He will use the lie of moderation to steal our people's sympathy. Then he will oppress us doubly. You did not know that?"

> "No," Princip said.

> "Even in our country the Prime Minister uses the lie of moderation to keep himself in power. Did you know that?"

> "I have heard of it."

> "Are you ready to fight such liars with all means?"

> "Yes."

These words were spoken in Sarajevo in 1914, at the Black Hand initiation ceremony in which a twenty-year-old Serb, Gavrilo Princip, was commissioned to murder Franz Ferdinand, heir to the Austro-Hungarian throne—thereby inciting World War I.

One hundred years later, disparaging the "lie of moderation" is still a favorite toxin of terrorists, talk radio, and spin doctors of every stripe. They have learned that demonizing the center works just as well for character assassination as it does for actual assassination. After all, moderation depends upon nuance and humility, both of which are the bane of extremists and the visceral manipulation that is their tradecraft. Frederic Morton knew something of this subject, having fled the Nazis in 1939.

According to the *New York Times Magazine*, at a Chicago rally for Bernie Sanders in March of 2020, teachers' union organizer Stacy Davis Gates warmed up the crowd by saying, "See, moderation is a dream killer," and "moderation is inhumane." Recall that during Hitler's rise, the Social Democrats begged the German Communist Party to join it in opposition to Nazism. The communists refused, dismissing the Social Democrats as despicable moderates. So where are we in the metastasis of extremism when the middle itself becomes the perceived evil? I'm not sure, but it's not good.

At this point, it's worth considering what the center is not. It is not an appeal for moral relativism. Evil is not a legitimate opposing truth to be balanced against something else. It is destructive at its very essence. Evil is loose in the world every day. Despots, terrorists, school shooters, and pedophiles are our daily reminders that evil is not simply the absence of good. Evil is an active, powerful, virulent force. Be assured that the center doesn't accommodate evil; it exposes it, letting truth compete with fear, loyalty, greed, and all the other arrows in evil's quiver that tend to silence reason.

And evil comes from the edges. It hates the moderate.

But all is not lost. There are sleeper cells of reason among us if you look for the clues that reveal them.

Consider this passage in David Brooks's *The Road to Character:*

> The stoic ideal holds that emotion should be distrusted more often than trusted. Emotion robs you of agency, so distrust desire. Distrust anger, and even sadness and grief...People in this mold try to control emotion with the firebreaks of decorum.

There's a clue. The *firebreaks of decorum*: manners, mutual respect, fighting fair. When we were children, we all asked our mothers why that stuff matters. Now we know. Disagreement escalates in their absence. How do we restore them?

The center is a product of the extremes that it defies. While an old expression teaches that "things in the middle of the road get run over," don't believe it. The center is not boring—it's where the real action is. The middle is much more dynamic than either magnetic pole because it is suspended between them. F. Scott Fitzgerald said that "the test of a first-rate intelligence is the ability to hold two opposed ideas in the mind at the same time." The fusion of colliding ideas creates its own truth.

If the extremes are the sharp edges of our society, cutting us apart, the middle is the constantly stitching needle. We have constructed sturdy seams through the genius of our political system and the invisible hand of the marketplace, both representing peaceful mechanisms to hold multiple thoughts simultaneously on just about everything. That weave has served Western civilization quite well. Contrast any authoritarian and militaristic societies with our own and you will recognize the dangers of any blind ideology as an organizing principle or economic model. Lord Acton said that power corrupts. My corollary is that rigid ideology corrupts also.

Undistorted public opinion on most persistent issues will express as a bell curve, just as with most other data sets (height, intelligence, religious belief, etc.). Bell curves are unsatisfying to those with the two diametrically opposed points of view on either end of a given distribution. They are the zealots who define the debate as they clash—whether in politics, sports, commerce, military, or spiritual matters. Breaking the bell curve is their objective, and they will use every available tactic to do so.

As Thomas Jefferson wrote to John Taylor in 1798, "In every free & deliberating society, there must from the nature of man be opposite parties, & violent dissentions & discords; and one of these for the most part must prevail over the other for a longer or shorter time."

Each point of view must have a champion—usually a leader with impressive historical knowledge, a sharp tongue, and a flair for motivation. These champions never call retreat, and they are both convinced and convincing when articulating their sacred extreme. They recast reality to suit their ends.

That approach works for a while, but the course of human events tends to humble the proud and the certain with astonishing regularity. COVID, for example, turned many doctrines on their head. Small government "no handouts" people in theory became big government "more bailouts" people in practice. Identity groups spun a feigned victimhood when the threat was more universal than discrete. If that intellectual flexibility brings humility and self-examination, it will be progress. If it doesn't have that effect, it will be naked hypocrisy.

Mo Gawdat, the former CEO of Google China, describes the ancient Chinese concept of yin and yang in Chinese philosophy this way:

> The duo yin and yang describe how apparently opposite forces are actually complementary, interconnected, and interdependent. Everything has both a yin, the feminine or negative principle...and a yang, the masculine or positive principle...For example, a shadow cannot exist without light, and vice versa. In a harmonious life, yin and yang complement each other. If you throw a stone in a lake, the waves will have troughs and peaks that calm each other down until the water is still again. To find a balanced life, one should embrace both sides and avoid the extremes of either.

The middle is neither limp nor static. As one extreme begins to yield or strengthen, the middle must constantly redefine itself, rebalancing within the new reality. Again, COVID moved the middle in many theaters of thought with a speed we had never experienced.

In most systems, equilibrium is the momentary Zen state, and balance is how we get there. The essential element is the healthy tension that makes the middle happen. Ask a gymnast if balance is difficult—or a business manager, an economist, a design engineer, a constitutional scholar, a chef, a military strategist, or anyone else who must make trade-offs between two or more essential forces in opposition. Difficult yes, but not optional. Failure is assured without it.

Balance requires qualities that hard data and clever rhetoric cannot provide: reason, judgment, and humanity. Our complicated world requires these attributes because only they can maintain equilibrium over time. Machine learning and data analytics are powerful disciplines, but they can only find quantitative correlations. The sacred algorithm that finds the center requires a very human tool kit.

America still communicates to the world that collective decisions made by the free will of individuals are the cornerstone of civilization and social advancement. By definition, democratic republics believe in "the wisdom of crowds." A recent bestseller by that name teases out some interesting proofs. If we don't actually believe in collective wisdom anymore, then the multicultural, multi-faith experiment of America these last two centuries will be nothing more than an ephemeral shooting star across the arc of human events. It's the difference between a durable alloy and a fading patchwork quilt.

If these "core of the center" organizing principles cannot hold, we will have only demonstrated the inevitability of prosperity's degradation into entitlement, jealousy, corruption, and oppression. This is an old lesson displayed anew that Karl Marx would relish from the grave.

But the centrist worldview has a big branding problem. Can we really glorify the middle of anything? Maybe a jelly doughnut has a middle worthy of praise, but aren't ideas in the conceptual middle just doomed to wallflower status at the ideology dance contest that cable news hath wrought? We may yearn for Reasoner and Cronkite, but how would they fare today in competition with Tucker Carlson and Rachel Maddow?

CHAPTER THREE

The Old Normal

In 1950, British philosopher and Nobel Prize–winner Bertrand Russell published an obscure collection of lectures and short-form writing called *Unpopular Essays*. Russell referred to himself as Third Earl Russell to tease his own aristocratic birth—and brought to the moderate position a force, style, and intellect the likes of which we have rarely seen since his death in 1970. Consider this excerpt:

> Our confused and difficult world needs various things if it is to escape disaster, and among these one of the most necessary is that, in the nations that still uphold Liberal beliefs, those beliefs should be wholehearted and profound, not apologetic towards dogmas of the right and of the left, but deeply persuaded of the value of liberty, scientific freedom, and mutual forbearance. For without those beliefs life on our politically divided but technically unified planet will hardly continue to be possible.

The word *liberal* in his day had a different meaning than it does today. For the Third Earl and his audience, it simply meant post-Enlightenment: a willingness to embrace progressive ideals around human rights and the advancement of scientific knowledge without religious oppression.

Who carries Third Earl Russell's mantle today? If you Google "Moderate Hall of Fame," there actually is such a thing at www. newmoderate.com/hall-of-fame. Alas, none of the anointed members are living people.

Even a casual look backward indicates that cooperation, consensus, and mutual respect are the best substrate for shared prosperity. The Greek philosophers described "the golden mean" as the desirable place between excess and deficiency. There are expansive charts that explore this Aristotelian concept across many personal attributes. For example, friendly is the mean between the excess of obsequiousness and the deficiency of cantankerousness, wittiness is the mean between the excess of buffoonery and the excess of boorishness, and so on. So this notion of balance seems stunningly obvious. Obvious at least until we watch fellow humans revert to single-minded tribal behaviors. When they feel challenged. When they feel powerful. When they get righteous. When the only truth is their own. What does seem new, perhaps, is that often the most comfortable people in our society are also the angriest.

One clue regarding our emotional trajectory might be found in a recent book, *The Decadent Society* by Ross Douthat, a thoughtful, conservative *New York Times* columnist. The book studies how our pre-COVID levels of comfort, safety, and wealth in America allowed us to indulge in a doom loop of cultural warfare. The global pandemic may have spawned an even uglier version of that cycle.

The blending of social disciplines that has had to occur to get us to this point has been underway for some time. In 1979, Jerry Falwell created the Moral Majority on the premise that those Christians who shared a set of traditional values and beliefs were politically and culturally powerless—and that they should band together to change that situation. The actual organization was disbanded in 1989, but wherever you reside on the political spectrum, you have to give credit to Reverend Falwell for striking a match near dry tinder.

As I write this in 2022, no one could accurately say that conservatives are powerless. *Roe v. Wade* has been overturned, delivering evangelicals their prized objective forty-three years after the Moral Majority began. Note that Reverend Falwell promoted his concept as centrist, determined to expose the self-protective cabal of institutional government that some now call the "deep state." As liberals rise up to meet that power, they also sell their movement as centrist. The loudest recent voice of their disfranchised majority is the aging impassioned socialist Bernie Sanders. Take some amusement from the irony that the fight club that is twenty-first century America features an array of radicals peddling what they each claim are mainstream ideals. The enablers in their respective media clans play along like reliable house organs.

An honest historian has trouble being an ideologue, though ideologues are frequently selective historians. History, we discover repeatedly, is a very practical animal. All sorts of unlikely alliances, muddle-through solutions, and seemingly impossible bedfellows occur routinely in the history of anything.

Absurdity is history's constant companion. Situations matter, and culture matters. Systems, technology, and politics matter. And clearly the X factor of leadership matters tremendously. One size doesn't fit all, so it's hard to look across the sweep of history and sustain purist positions like "demography is destiny," "economic forces are always deterministic," or "the world always turns on personalities and leadership." All these things are true—but only in their turn. They make good icebreakers for dinner parties or topics for term papers, but little more when the biggest, most difficult issues are in play.

FRENEMIES

When we examine history's most spirited rivals, it is instructive to note the way in which many of their personal journeys end. The champions of opposing ideologies frequently become wizened by life's experience, tempering their grip on once cherished absolutes. Late in life, they often find respect for their once despised enemies. John Adams and Thomas Jefferson's well-chronicled tender exchange of letters in the twilight of their years is the most celebrated American reconciliation. After the two battled for years in their prime, Adams's last words were "Thomas Jefferson lives." That both men died on the same day, July 4, fifty years to the day from the definitive statement of American independence, is hard to ignore if you suspect divine coincidences in history.

There is magic in reconciliation, forgiveness, and respect.

When Sir Winston Churchill said of his intellectual rivals, "I like a man who grins when he fights," he was conceding that there is a healthy measure of theater resident in all of our strident advocacies—most especially there were in his. Grudging respect for our opponents comes from that essential self-awareness. Even zealots tend to lose their invective in the fullness of time. Proof, if you need it, rests in Churchill's reconciliation with his bitter foe Neville Chamberlain.

As Chamberlain lay dying after resigning from the war cabinet in September 1940, Churchill wrote the former prime minister to "express to you my admiration for the heroic effort you have made to do your duty and to see this grim business through, and my sincere sorrow that, with nerve unshaken and mental prowess unimpaired, your physical strength no longer bears you up in a public station." He added, "I have greatly valued our comradeship and your aid and counsel during these five violent months, and I beg you to believe me your sincere friend." In the midst of German bombs and strategic difficulties that fall, Churchill wrote thoughtful updates to Chamberlain and offered to show him confidential documents about the war effort.

Two days after Chamberlain died on November 19, Churchill wrote Chamberlain's widow:

> During these long violent months of war we had come closer together than at any time in our twenty years of friendly relationship amid the ups & downs of politics. I greatly admired his fortitude and firmness of spirit. I felt when I served under him that he [would] never give in: & I knew when our positions were reversed that I [could] count upon the aid of a loyal and unflinching comrade.

There are many more such reconciliations both here and abroad: F.W. de Klerk and Nelson Mandela, pioneering heart surgeons Michael DeBakey and Denton Cooley, Bill Clinton and George

H. W. Bush. Great leaders in the autumn of their years often confirm their greatness by acquiring humility around once strident positions. Their final gift to history is a measured reflection on their own views and, ultimately, respect for their ideological opponents.

Charles Darwin, after battling creationism for decades, in his later years developed a convincing religious belief. He didn't have to abandon science; he just gave enough ground to accommodate spirituality. He found both could coexist. As between great figures of history, the middle can win in the end. Yeats notwithstanding, the center *can* hold. The golden mean is always out there.

Balance and compromise are, to say the least, unfashionable topics in public discourse at present. We could even say that extremist circles actively scorn those qualities. So it is hardly surprising that modern practitioners of the moderate arts aren't power players.

Wise, capable legislative mechanics once inspired reverence for their talents. Like master chefs, people celebrated them for their ability to combine disparate elements and juggle volatile personalities to execute a delectable result. Leverage, timing, a dash of treat, a pinch of vanity, false modesty—their skills were unabashedly practical. Examples include Bob Dole, Howard Baker, Sam Nunn, Robert Taft, and the great compromiser of the 1700s, Henry Clay. In their time, their peers recognized them as leaders of the first order. Who is famous for consensus building today?

I can't think of anyone, except maybe the Argentine Pope. Is it ironic that a Catholic pontiff, a figure whose job involves propagation of a particular ideology, could be the leading voice of the middle? Not really is the answer, because it's not actually as surprising as it might sound. Christianity itself is the ultimate alloy. As we will see in Chapter 7, members of the clergy must constantly apply opposing truths to do their job effectively.

CHAPTER FOUR

The Siren Song of the Extreme

There is no general doctrine which is not capable of eating out our morality if unchecked by a deep-seated habit of direct fellow-feeling with individual fellow-men.

—GEORGE ELIOT, *MIDDLEMARCH*

The lure of extreme positions is easy to grasp: they can be succinctly expressed, are pithy and therefore media-friendly, and are savory in their simplicity. Dogmatists and ideologues rant evangelically from either side of an argument, talking past each other without hope of—or desire for—reconciliation. After all, they each peddle certainty, and certainty is a salve that calms the mind and emboldens the spirit. We naturally search for it like junkies craving our next fix.

George Will, in *The Conservative Sensibility,* describes our condition thusly,

Some people who fancy themselves intellectually emancipated—who think themselves liberated from what they call a stultifying cultural inheritance—actually reside in what G. K. Chesterton called "the clean, well-lit prison of one idea."

The lead-in narrative for any dogma will claim that the center is a cop-out. "If you don't believe in something, then you will fall for anything" is the extremist's opening gambit to discredit the notion of compromise. Notice the rhetorical sleight of hand, as if the center weren't something you could *believe* in. Well, I do, and fervently.

If you fail to dispute an extremist's initial proposition, then you can only *believe* in the simple, crisp answers of packaged ideology. Facts, empirical history, and individual circumstances be damned, because only their version of a rules-based society can prevail. Each side wants to control the rules. The alternative involves doing the work of building relationships and listening—acknowledging difficult trade-offs to meet opponents where they are, issue by issue, situation by situation.

George Eliot's observation about "general doctrines" sounds so civilized, but we now understand the incivility that follows. Viruses of the mind propagate with almost biological predictability. Research on the timing of neurons in the parts of the brain that govern instinct and reason show that we tend to start with a loyalty or a conclusion and then cherry-pick arguments and evidence to defend it.

In *The Brothers Karamazov*, Fyodor Dostoevsky summed up the human penchant for ideological subservience when he wrote, "There is no more ceaseless or tormenting care for man, as long as he remains free, than to find someone to bow down to as soon as possible"—in the case of the novel, the Grand Inquisitor.

We say we crave freedom, yet still we yearn for the comfort of simple edicts issued by strong men or women. Paul Valéry expressed that thought succinctly in 1895, "The folly of mistaking a paradox for a discovery, a metaphor for a proof, a torrent of verbiage for a spring of capital truths, and oneself for an oracle, is inborn in us."

Alas, loyalty stops being a virtue when it requires abandoning individual reason. The center demands learning and compromise, which are impossible without education, exposure, and enlightenment. To quote Thomas Jefferson, "if a nation expects to be both ignorant & free, in a state of civilization, it expects what never was & never will be."

That observation begs an explanation of the Dunning-Kruger effect, named after Cornell University psychologists David Dunning and Justin Kruger, who posited that people who know the least are the most confident in their opinions. *Psychology Today* summarizes this theory as follows:

> The Dunning-Kruger effect is a cognitive bias in which people wrongly overestimate their knowledge or ability in a specific area. This tends to occur because a lack of self-awareness prevents them from accurately assessing their skills.

The psychologists published the results of a study that "tested participants on their logic, grammar, and sense of humor, and found that those who performed in the bottom quartile rated their skills far above average." The research suggests that people struggle with *metacognition*. In other words, the underperformers were incompetent both in the direct task at hand and in self-reflecting to recognize that incompetence. "Those with limited knowledge in a domain suffer a dual burden: Not only do they reach mistaken conclusions and make regrettable errors, but their incompetence robs them of the ability to realize it," the researchers wrote. For example, those in the 12th percentile self-rated their expertise to be, on average, in the 62nd percentile.

Psychology Today continues:

> The Dunning-Kruger effect has been found in domains ranging from logical reasoning to emotional intelligence, financial knowledge, and firearm safety. And the effect isn't spotted only among incompetent individuals; most people have weak points where the bias can take hold. It also applies to people with a seemingly solid knowledge base: Individuals rating as high as the 80th percentile for a skill have still been found to overestimate their ability to some degree.
>
> This tendency may occur because gaining a small amount of knowledge in an area about which one was previously ignorant can make them feel as though they're suddenly virtual experts. Only after continuing to explore a topic do people often realize how extensive it is and how much they still have to master.

Dunning and Kruger nicely explained the internet's effect on popular psychology more than two decades ago. The small screens in our hands are catnip that feeds our addiction to general doctrines. A little information is a dangerous thing. No one was surprised when the *Wall Street Journal* quoted from an internal Facebook presentation in 2018 that stated, "Our algorithms exploit the human brain's attraction to divisiveness" and "if left unchecked" would feed users "more and more divisive content in an effort to gain user attention & increase time on the platform."

The *Journal* also cites a 2016 presentation that examined groups "swamped with racist, conspiracy-minded and pro-Russian content," finding that "64% of their joins are due to our recommendation tools." Nothing much has changed at Facebook. Confirmation bias is a core part of any social media platform's business strategy.

Long before Dunning and Kruger, Carl Jung was correct when he declared, "People don't have ideas. Ideas have people." Brain science, sociological research, and the field of psychology have affirmed Jung, Eliot, and Dunning and Kruger over and over. Dogma peddlers of every stripe pour a heady elixir: no more reasoning is necessary, no more learning, listening, or taxing judgment—just *action* in the name of *certainty* to advance the great cause. Tolerance without diversity, diversity without tolerance: it's all paint by numbers. Whether the dogmatist is pro-ISIS, pro-life, anti-fascist, or a radical environmentalist, the tactics and the rhetoric are almost always the same. Create a false choice, erect a straw man, extrapolate from a dramatic anecdote, spread fear with impunity, and repeat.

We marvel at the targeted media weapons extremists have at their disposal today, but before we mourn the futility of reason, let's mention the phenomenon that is Jordan Peterson. If you don't know of Dr. Peterson, you probably aren't between the ages of eighteen and thirty-five. He is a clinical psychologist and college professor at the University of Toronto who has had to go to court to avoid dismissal from his teaching post, given that the intolerant culture of academia has deemed his views politically incorrect. That situation isn't remarkable. What *is* remarkable is his wild popularity among liberal-leaning millennials.

There is nothing slick, flashy, or produced about Dr. Peterson, yet his YouTube channel has 5.79 million subscribers, and his Twitter account has 2.9 million followers. Whether you agree with Dr. Peterson's views or not, it's worth noting that his weapon is reason alone. Logic and factual data are his only currencies. No fear, no sex, no greed—no victim complex or appeal to emotion. He even defies our modern craving for brevity. Dr. Peterson is often long-winded and arcane, which should be anathema to our shrinking attention spans, but his social awkwardness seems part of his appeal.

The *Wall Street Journal* and many other publications have tried to explain his unlikely celebrity among otherwise progressive young people, and it may come down to Caitlin Flanagan's simple observation in *The Atlantic*: "What they were getting from these lectures and discussions…was perhaps the only sustained argument against identity politics they had heard in their lives."

In Dr. Peterson's world, the antinomy is between individual responsibility and group identity. That's not a new idea; many moderate statesmen have eloquently contrasted freedom and responsibility in society, preferring less or more of one or the other. However, many young adults have apparently never heard it before, and a clunky appeal to reason is turning their heads—a promising sign. Unless we actively seek the balance of consensus, extreme belief is easier than a life that examines itself, questions its own motives, and considers that it may benefit from the opinions of others.

Perhaps the hardest lesson for most of us to learn is that people feel the way they feel—full stop. I wince as I remember my wonkish twenties, when I was certain that I could change people's minds with facts and the power of logic. I have learned that facts are less of a determinant of human behavior than emotions. Jonathan Haidt is a popular psychologist who describes the human condition as akin to a logical rider atop an emotional elephant. The rider appears to be in charge, but when he and the elephant disagree, the elephant will have its way. When confronted with our emotional elephant, psychiatrists cite two phenomena: cognitive dissonance and confirmation bias.

Cognitive dissonance is the discomfort that we feel amid conflicting information and arguments, leading to our tendency to seek consistency, even when it requires us to ignore important facts. Marketers know this instinct all too well. Cognitive dissonance occurs routinely at the grocery store when clever packaging gets us to spend more on a brand-name product, even when we know the less expensive generic item beside it is essentially the same. This tendency deeply influences all our decisions. Watch focus groups and note how quickly logic gets lost. The best trial lawyers understand cognitive dissonance and can create an alternate universe in the courtroom to exploit it. They are supremely talented elephant trainers.

Confirmation bias is the trusty weapon of cognitive dissonance: once we form a point of view, we routinely accept facts that support that notion and reject facts that undermine it. Hence, the Feynman principle, named after Nobel Prize–winning physicist

Richard Feynman: "You must not fool yourself [because] you are the easiest person to fool."

What do these principles have to do with the middle, you ask? *Everything* is the answer, because the healthy, mature brain must learn to struggle with competing factors (price, risk, affinity, etc.) if it is to override natural tendencies. Insanity in its literal daily expression is not the state of imbalance but the failure to seek it. Or as G. K. Chesterton noted, "What embitters the world is not excess of criticism, but an absence of self-criticism."

That statement should obviously trigger introspection. In that regard, I have considered that my fascination with the middle may be just my own cognitive dissonance supercharged by my own reinforcement bias. But I do take Chesterton's words to heart and practice self-criticism methodically. A larger question is whether I will do so publicly in a way that challenges those around me.

The 2018 bestseller *Factfulness*, by Hans Rosling, convincingly demonstrated that even the brightest among us default to pessimistic conclusions rather than appreciating the progress all around us. So are people inherently irrational if the brain is naturally more receptive to bad news than good news?

Well, let's just say that we can all be stubbornly illogical until the weight of logical evidence becomes overwhelming enough to override both cognitive dissonance and reinforcement bias. At that moment, the center can move with astonishing speed, in the "tipping point" phenomenon made famous by Malcolm Gladwell in his volume by the same name. Jordan Peterson's popularity may represent something of a tipping point, a moment when the middle must furiously recalculate itself. COVID is a middle-mover across multiple dimensions. You might also ask deposed despots how quickly everything can change—many times, they don't survive long enough to answer the question.

If it is generally a little event or idea that pushes sentiment on any given issue over the edge, how can we know which little thing matters most? After all, it has become an article of faith that we shouldn't "sweat the small stuff." Sometimes we should. But when, exactly?

When experts examine a plane crash, a battle, or a pandemic, they can generally determine, in hindsight, which little factor most affected the overall outcome. Real-time analysis is much harder. Are there clues? I don't have a crisp formula other than to say we know that people learn from stories. Change often has a face. Joe Posnanski said of baseball player Stan Musial that his was a big story of little stories, small kindnesses, and quiet dignity. Tonality, respect, and the way we make people feel are the original influencers. Instinctively, great leaders know which little things move the middle.

Cold-eyed marketers maintain that most human behaviors are traceable to one of the three primary motivators: fear, sex, and greed. Notice that reason and logic didn't make the short list. There is plenty of evidence for that worldview, but many powerful human events haven't stemmed from those three factors. Charity and goodness, for example, can't be explained by the marketer's playbook. We know that little things—like opening a door for a stranger, flashing a smile, saying a kind word, or asking about your coworker's family—benefit both parties. Fortunately, our actual list of motivators is more complex than the marketers believe.

Consider, perhaps, that decency is the fourth primary motivator. Alexis de Tocqueville, author of the enduring masterpiece *Democracy in America*, is often credited with prophesizing that America will only be a great nation so long as it is a good nation. The fourth motivator, in other words, is the most important one. Good is an alloy forged from decency. Good is a social form of antimony. Good is comfortable with definition by its enemies, and its enemies are ideological warriors of every stripe. The only American exceptionalism that matters is how we treat each other.

CHAPTER FIVE

Of Media, Markets, and the Gerrymander

One of the most persistent delusions of mankind is that some sections of the human race are morally better or worse than the others. This belief has many forms, none of which has any rational basis.

—BERTRAND RUSSELL

A prominent, much-decorated journalist told me once that "it's well understood in my profession that the best way to advance your career is to take down a great man." Absorb that for a moment, and then ask yourself why we lack heroes in today's cultural landscape. You likely have noticed that a nonpartisan, traditional broadsheet media property does not fit well into that landscape. Those properties are increasingly organized as nonprofits. They will still compete for funding, just in a different realm than subscription or advertiser-supported properties.

THE PROFESSIONAL BLAME GAME

"The Media" is ever a handy whipping boy for all that ails us, and like most allegations, there would be some evidence to support that view if we ever agreed on what or who The Media is. Whatever it is, we do know this much: as newsprint has given way to pixels, our attention span has shortened. This shift has, in turn, pressured all media to find a niche audience, and provocation offers the simplest method to do that.

We can decide to condemn the media, the internet, or anything else, but does it ultimately matter who is at fault? Even if we could make supportable conclusions, they'd only lead us down a blind alley to the negativism that got us here. And as we have learned, negativism is a self-reinforcing behavior. We won't find the center that way. Solutions do require some recognition of the causative factors, but the more interesting question is where we go from here.

Like most social inquiries, this one should start in the mirror. If the news media and social media platforms have helped aggravate our angry mindset, it's because we watched. Fox News monetized the same backlash that Falwell tapped into decades earlier. Any discussion about media needs to recognize a basic segmentation between produced media (professional media) and spontaneous media (me media).

Bertrand Russell had this to say about professional media:

> It is natural to think well of ourselves, and thence, if our mental processes are simple, of our sex, our class, our nation, and our age. But among writers, especially moralists, a less direct expression of self-esteem is common. They tend to think ill of their neighbors

and acquaintances, and therefore to think well of the sections of mankind to which they themselves do not belong.

When media was a centralized affair, William Randolph Hearst and Joseph Pulitzer practiced the sweeping, simplistic good-versus-evil themes of yellow journalism because they worked to attract readers and revenue. And news outlets still do. Clickbait headlines are all about provocation and temptation. For the corporate media, stoking fights remains an easy bang-for-your-buck recipe. White men of privilege are the safest targets, even as ownership of corporate media rapidly reconsolidates in the hands of typically white and male Hearsts and Pulitzers of our day.

But any criticism of corporate media becomes a long look in Third Earl Russell's mirror. If most modern writers are moralists, we the audience have made them so. To change the media supply, we first have to change our demand. The genius of Roger Ailes and Rush Limbaugh is that they found a missing, loud voice that resonated against the real bias of the "mainstream media." They played to our own hardwired biases, and we responded. They got paid. The middle shrank. Instead of trimming their sails toward the middle, both the media establishment and its right-wing challengers became righteous and indignant. The middle shrank further.

ME MEDIA

In the early days, the internet seemed to offer the promise of democratizing information, dethroning media gatekeepers, and supporting the proliferating citizen publishers. Those changes actually happened, but the results are not the idyllic individual empowerment many had hoped for.

As Ryan Holiday said in a recent podcast, "Stories are a wonderful way to learn about the lives of others, but they are a terrible way to live." Projecting oneself into a constructed narrative has always represented a form of egocentric "big me" delusion, but with social media, the imaginary audience has become real. So instead of being a player in an electronic construct like *FarmVille* or *Second Life* (baby steps on the path to full-on e-hedonism), you can be your own emoji, living an actual superficial life instead of an imagined one. The fast cars and the private planes don't have to be yours; the selfie is what matters.

There is a phenomenon in psychotherapy known as the "hedonistic paradox," which states that the best way to avoid happiness is to seek it too directly. Social media encourages that unhealthy tendency while pulling us away from focusing on others or our commonality. Social media has not been an instrument of reason; it is no friend of those who seek the center.

THE VOTING RIGHTS ACT

Psychology notwithstanding, the mechanics of democracy are where choices get made in a free society, and how those mechanics change as technology progresses and regional demographics evolve. Every positive step in one generation has to be examined to see whether it is still positive in a changed social context. The Voting Rights Act of 1965 has powerful symbolism surrounding it such that it is hard to question it without appearing to question its noble pretense, but we must. As we ponder causation, the process of reapportionment, also known as redistricting, is an issue few beyond political insiders discuss. However, gerrymandering by both parties tends to reward incumbents and the most partisan candidates. Because primaries are the gateway to the general election, candidates must "play to the base" in the spring if they want to be on the ballot in the fall. In Texas, for example, there are twenty-two million voters, but only two million vote in the Republican primary—so just over one million voters can nominate the winner in November. No Democrat has won statewide since 1994.

For all its virtue, the Voting Rights Act of 1965 didn't help mitigate this phenomenon—and likely made it worse. Even progressives now whisper among themselves that they should weigh its usefulness against its unintended consequences. A few states have taken the task of reapportionment away from officeholders, which is a big step in the right direction.

The existing process results in elected public officials who are no longer transactional, in the sense of hammering out the important business of government. They get elected by flaunting their anger—and have no incentive to operate differently once elected. Those who do become transactional almost automatically attract attacks from the left or right. The proliferation of 501(c)(4) "dark money" organizations fuels that pattern because financial anonymity and extremism are natural allies.

Several states are reconsidering their reapportionment process to reclaim the middle in representative districts. Extremists of every stripe oppose those reforms, which should tell you all you need to know about their value. Ranked-choice voting is another increasingly popular methodology that may prove helpful in reclaiming the middle. The "let's raise and spend enough to make the runoff" tactic tends to reward the more extreme candidates.

FINANCIAL MARKETS

Before we leave causation, let's consider the nerve center of capitalism, what most call Wall Street. Ideally, markets provide access to capital and liquidity to those who deserve it, while punishing those who use other people's money irresponsibly. We have traveled some distance from that ideal, and the public knows it. Obscene CEO pay packages, high-speed trading, derivatives such as credit default swaps, and opaque shell-game securitizations have increasingly exposed Wall Street as an insider's game.

The pattern is clear: the "haves" tend to either get rich or get bailed out, and the "have-nots" get stimulus checks to purchase their silence. Even the wisest winners in the game have quietly started to wonder whether the decline of meritocracy in the market is defensible. Technology and information reward those with access to them. The middle class, along with the middle in politics and society, shrinks as that advantage compounds. The digital divide is about much more than bandwidth.

CHAPTER SIX

A Field Guide to the Middle All around Us

When I think of one, I prefer the other.

—A FRENCH MORALIST COMMENTING ON THE
CHARACTER OF VOLTAIRE AND ROUSSEAU

Let's take a journey to the practical center as it operates within our daily lives, amid competing philosophies of governance and commerce, religion, man-made structures, military science, genomics, monetary policy, and corporate operating models.

THE BUILT ENVIRONMENT

Architects and engineers live by two very different clichés. Ludwig Mies van der Rohe, the brilliant architect, famously asserted that "God is in the details," yet we also commonly hear from our friends in engineering and hard sciences that "the devil is in the details." Who is right? They both are. Soaring cathedrals testify to the glory of the builder's art, but the ability of an edifice to withstand the test of time and exposure to the elements requires minute structural calculations. Only by merging the two can a reliable building rise from the earth. Elegant trade-offs are a given for those who succeed in any field of applied design.

Harriet Monroe said of architect William Prettyman, "His genius was betrayed by lofty and indomitable traits of character which could not yield or compromise. And so his life was a tragedy of inconsequence." Unlike Prettyman, we generally don't have any trouble accepting the practical necessities of compromise between form and function. But when considering trade-offs between ideals such as individual liberty and collective security, things get more contentious.

THE MIDDLE IN SPORT

Some say sports are the candy store of life, which I take to mean sport is the proxy for all our satisfying dramas. War can serve that purpose, too, but it causes people to die, making for a more complicated metaphor. Like a jar of sweets on the shelf, our sports interests allow us to pick our favorite team, players, or games and savor the delirious collective advocacy known as "fandom." Every game day, we get to participate emotionally in the sweetness of victory and the sour taste of defeat—all inside a harmless alternate reality.

Let's take that concept a step further to find the antinomy. Fandom can simply mean blind allegiance to a team, but most knowledgeable sports fans have a philosophical point of view about their game. Football fans, for example, tend to cluster around platitudes such as "defense wins championships" or "there's no substitute for speed (or time of possession, or the kicking game)." Every sport has its conceptual refrains. They keep the verbal competition going long after the field lights have turned off. Conveniently, there is always plenty of evidence to support each point of view. So who is right? Do we even want an answer? It turns out we all get to be right, which is lovely.

But what about discovering a whole new antinomy? In *Moneyball*, Michael Lewis does a wonderful job of telling the story of the Oakland A's under manager Billy Beane. Beane didn't adopt one of the established "pitching-centric" or "hitting-centric" philosophies. Instead, he rejected both and cast his lot with a whole new way of thinking that involved avoided outs, assigning quantitative values to team outcomes that flowed from previously underappreciated individual behaviors. Lurking within the statistics of the most statistically analyzed game in human history was a new truth.

New truths tend to have a hard time entering the citadel of popular thinking generally, but perhaps even more so in baseball. Nothing is more unsettling than hearing that your cherished position and your traditional opponent's point of view are demonstrably untrue. For baseball (and increasingly basketball, soccer, and other sports), *Moneyball* moved the middle in an important way.

MICROECONOMICS

If every building is a monument to the middle, and if every sport requires a delicate chemistry of inputs, then economics expresses the same idea through a concept any sophomore student of the subject knows well: diminishing marginal returns.

That law states that the marginal output of a production process will decrease as the amount of a single factor of production incrementally increases, when the amounts of all other factors of production stay constant. In other words, balance is highly important in any economic system. Not only will amounts of any input—say, the number of workers on an assembly line—improve results less and less with each new increase, they will eventually *diminish* those results. With apologies to "Never Too Much" singer Luther Vandross, too much of anything is not good for you.

In *David and Goliath*, Malcom Gladwell describes the "inverted U curve" in various contexts beyond economics to demonstrate diminishing marginal returns. That curve depicts some measure of success on the Y-axis and some input measure on the X-axis. In one example, he confronts the notion that the lowest possible student–teacher ratio is desirable in an educational setting. Gladwell cites research indicating that fewer than nine children per teacher in a classroom actually *hurts* academic performance. It turns out kids learn from each other, not just from the teacher.

Even inputs that have proven value can become damaging if overused. So here we are, back at balance and equilibrium.

BIOLOGY

These principles align with what we know about genomics. The "nature versus nurture" debate has raged in sociology, biology, and parlor gossip for centuries. The "nature" side argues we are slaves to our genetic makeup and we can't substantively change our potential or innate tendencies beyond that biological reality. The "nurture" side argues that the parenting, education, coaching, and mentorship we receive represent the most important factors in our individual outcomes.

As we learned to decode the genome, the "nature" extremists felt pretty flush. The wet software of our DNA was about to explain all human foibles, gifts, and differences.

Then along came epigenetics, an increasingly accepted scientific discipline that says, darn it, it's just not that simple. Genes are less determinant than their expression, which is greatly affected by events, environment, and habits. In other words, the middle strikes again. Nature is determinative until it's not, and nurture hits the same wall when we ask too much of it as a decoder of the past or future. All roads lead back to those words we love to hate: *it depends.*

Hybrid vigor is defined as "the increase in certain characteristics like growth rate, size, fertility, yield, etc. of a particular hybrid organism over its parents." That phenomenon is also known by some other names, including *heterosis* and *inbreeding enhancement.* Hybrid vigor occurs because the genetic contributions of the parents mix to enhance the offspring's traits. Stated simply, in genetics, diversity wins. Ask a farmer or a rancher about the power of genetic combination. Or ask Tiger Woods, Barack Obama, or Steph Curry.

MANAGEMENT SCIENCE

A common dilemma in any institution is the struggle between centralized authority and distributed authority. This is true in a government agency, a corporation, a nonprofit, or an information technology network. Each system offers benefits. Centralized authority often provides uniformity, strategic coherence, accountability at the top, and, in most cases, some perception of security. Decentralized systems offer empowerment on the front lines, nimbleness of reaction, accountability at the lower echelons, and the ability to learn from varied local circumstances.

Any organization, as it scales, faces the exact same "powerful hub versus powerful spokes" dilemma. All new chief executives want to impose their vision using different formulas for enterprise risk management and individual flexibility. For example, the need to secure corporate networks against cyberattack pulls in one direction, and the need to trust regional managers pulls in the other. Organizational equilibrium is elusive. Variables change, so in the best organizations, ideologies yield to realities.

Military culture celebrates its standardized rules while seeking to equip field personnel to make decisions in the absence of perfect information. In their world, the consequences of not acting can be fatal. Waiting for perfect information from headquarters would neuter military power. Perfect information simply happens too late, or never. The military has chosen a middle way and made that fusion work.

Similarly, in business, there is often more than one right decision. The quality of the execution post-decision becomes more important than the path chosen. Overinclusive, group-grope, paralysis-by-analysis processes often never get to the execution phase, waiting for more "buy-in" before choosing a path forward. We all remember the canard "a camel is a horse built by committee."

Mindless bureaucracy is the epitome of process run amok,

where procedures intended to mitigate the risk of criticism end up smothering any sense of a desired outcome. In theory, this approach drives "consistency"—which is, by definition, the sworn enemy of situational judgment. Churchill famously observed, "It is better to be both right and consistent. But if you have to choose—you must choose to be right."

During Steve Jobs's initial tenure as founder, and after his triumphant return, Apple had no executive decision-making process beyond his raw, mercurial instinct. Apple without Steve Jobs was a company of process and predictability, yet devoid of a creative genius. And we know which approach was more successful. So should we just find a brilliant leader and ignore all processes?

Well, let's see where that path takes us. When you fly, aren't you glad the pilot has a rote checklist to follow for every takeoff and landing? Should surgical suites have strict sterilization protocols or just improvise? Should judges and bureaucrats consider precedent or act on their momentary inspiration? We all want "due process" from certain types of organizations, and we get it—even if to a fault.

Different organizations, and even the same organization at different times, require a careful balance between process at the core and decisiveness at the edge. This calculation is the very art of management. One size never fits all.

We need defined processes, structure, and opportunity to create consensus around a given decision, but we also need courage and leadership. Strong leaders often have sharp edges, and the empirical evidence is overwhelming that taking all the sharp edges out of an organization to create a woke Valhalla means no one's feelings will get hurt—but the best people will also leave, along with the chance to align an urgent culture with shared goals. You will, in effect, create a government agency. So every organization needs a mixture of local initiative and centralized process.

Recall that our first go at fashioning a governing document for America was the Articles of Confederation, a scheme that, for a decade, proved too weak. That outcome was perhaps predictable, given that we had gone to war regarding centralized English authority over remote British territories. The next iteration, our Constitution, rebalanced the formula with supreme but enumerated powers at the federal level, restrained by a Bill of Rights that designated certain individual civil liberties as inviolate. The founders knew we needed power distributed in some tension with itself, but it took practical experience to refine the proper balance among the components.

Debate recurs at the Supreme Court year after year to get that balance right. We tinker with that balance at our peril. You may have noticed that Congress in the modern age doesn't concern itself with limitations on federal power. One reason is that, since the passage of the Seventeenth Amendment, Congress has no real structural incentive to restrain itself.

The Seventeenth Amendment radically modified the way we elect our United States Senate. Our Constitution designed a bicameral Congress with senators chosen by state legislatures. The Grange movement, and the Populist Party it spawned, succeeded in amending the Constitution in 1913 to elect senators by popular vote, just like members of the House of Representatives.

By eliminating the role of state governments in Washington, we damaged a carefully designed tension between the extremities and the core that the Constitutional Convention in Philadelphia had carefully designed. The horizontal "checks and balances" between the federal branches are cold comfort against the loss of state governments' seat at the table.

Senate campaigns were not meant to be the oversized house races they have become, driven by big money, direct mail, and pollsters. Aspiring senators were to have an electorate of a few hundred state legislators to whom they had to pledge allegiance to the federalist ideal of limited constitutional powers for the central government. How would Washington be different if that configuration remained?

Recall that the "popular election" of senators was meant to empower citizens directly. In actuality, it severed any hope for federalism—surely the bitterest of all unintended consequences across American history (Prohibition being a possible second, but that's for another time).

The bitter irony of many "populist" victories is that they often lead to outcomes that move power further from the people who wanted the change. We can praise our visionary forefathers who fashioned our Constitution, or we can embrace the Seventeenth Amendment, but we can't do both. Politically, there is no going back. The intended balance is lost. Power has centralized, meaning Washington can print money with impunity and then spend it or withhold it without regard for state sovereignty or enumerated powers.

MONETARY POLICY

Monetary policy is generally a nerd zone. It is only a dark art because so few are genuinely interested in it. Yet it deserves careful attention. Twice in the last thirteen years, the US Federal Reserve has had to save the world, functionally elevating it to the fourth branch of government. During the financial crisis of 2018, the Fed needed to save us from financial markets, and in 2020, from COVID.

Our central bank, the third version of itself in American history, operates under a "dual mandate." Its first goal is price stability, and the second is full employment. Those goals are usually in conflict. If other factors are constant, the marginal dollar of money supply created to juice the economy will be the same marginal dollar that devalues the currency and ignites inflation. Our Federal Reserve is the only major central bank in the world that must embrace that tension. So is the Fed doomed to failure? The answer is yes, but only if you view both elements of its mandate as absolutes. Balance is possible even if perfection is elusive. The trade-off between priorities is precisely what makes monetary policy interesting.

Fed watchers divide members of the Federal Open Market Committee into hawks, who are primarily inflation-sensitive, and doves, who are primarily focused on employment. We need them both.

The reactive, easy monetary policy known as "quantitative easing" allowed the Federal Reserve to grow its balance sheet from $800 million in September of 2008 to more than $4.2 trillion during the following twenty-four months to prop up corporate America and its poor credit decisions, even as the

Fed's actions had an enormously negative effect on the conservative retiree.

What happened in 2020 in response to a nonmarket event called COVID-19 dwarfed all that came before. Even the hawks became dovish, because there are moments when ideology has to accommodate reality. Did they sell out their convictions, or did they simply have the courage to adapt to circumstances? Maybe they would rather be right than be consistent. The good news is most of the world is pulling for the Fed to win its huge bluff because the moral hazard this time would be failing to save employment and small businesses. In 2022, the hawks' time came round at last; endless stimulus created demand outstripping supply, bringing back inflation with a vengeance.

RED AND BLUE

You might fairly ask at this point whether the dominant political parties represent an antinomy. The answer is clearly no, because antinomies involve opposing truths, and neither party stands for anything permanent enough to qualify. For example, in the 2020 election, both presidential nominees reversed their personal positions on abortion. One was a major Democratic contributor until he became the face of the Republican Party. There are no longer procedural norms in Congress that both parties agree to live by. Do a Google search for "can a president nominate a Supreme Court justice during the fourth year of a term?" and you will discover a stark recent example.

There are a number of playful YouTube videos in which an interviewer presents a person on the street with a political position of one candidate, while falsely attributing it to their opponent.

Without fail, the interviewee defends or disagrees with that idea according to their support for (or opposition to) the attributed candidate. As we have learned by now, blind allegiance is more the norm than the exception, so we can't claim surprise. But one can easily feel some empathy for the stooge in the video, because there are no longer many discernable core principles within either party.

In *Why We're Polarized*, Ezra Klein provides an interesting treatment of the idea that, with two political parties, "negative partisanship" has grown to the point that neither party can hold itself accountable to positive ideas. Protest voting is now just how we vote.

The COVID pandemic put the parties' intellectual flexibility on display at a scale much larger than ever before. Red-state leaders wanted federal dollars just as much as blue-state leaders, sidelining deficit hawks. Globalists and free traders self-quarantined their own ideas. Grover Norquist, a proponent of the lower-tax, smaller-government Republican cause, famously said he intended to elect candidates who would "shrink government down to the size where we can drown it in the bathtub." But once the government regained its status as an economic savior during the pandemic, exactly none of the "small government" people rejected federal dollars.

There are clearly moments when capitalism falters, leaving government as the investor of last resort. Ready examples are the New Deal programs of the thirties, emergency aid to the airline industry after 9/11, the 2008 bailout of the financial establishment, and the auto industry rescue of 2009. Libertarian dogmatists tend to become very quiet in the moments that require crude-but-necessary government solutions. Afterward, they do not long remember that, in a pinch, the practical center was more useful than any extremist hashtag. It is both pitiful and predictable that the decentralized finance ("DeFi") crowd is calling for better regulatory oversight now that they have seen the ugly aftermath of a financial free-for-all.

Extremist notions that can't weather extreme situations are useless by definition. So the "free markets know best" crowd and the "government knows best" crowd will both have to eat crow eventually. Because, you guessed it, the right answer is both—a thoughtful combination of the two ideas, depending on the circumstances. And if that sounds like work, it is. Political rhetoric is easy; governing is hard. Recall the lesson of Dunning and Kruger: the most strongly held opinions come from those least informed.

Easy answers aren't inherently wrong—they just tend to be.

CHAPTER SEVEN

Christian Theology and the Middle

There is in Jesus Christ a conjunction of such really diverse excellencies as otherwise would have seemed to us utterly incompatible on the same subject...both wonderfully meet in him.

—JONATHAN EDWARDS

As with many big questions, religion may be the best screen on which to project the panoramic idea of opposing truths that are both true yet always in a tenuous equilibrium.

I will speak of Christian faith because that's what I know best. Salt and light provide the Bible's primary metaphor for what one author has called the double helix of Christian faith. They represent the relationship between truth and grace. Grace is the kindness, encouragement, and charity prescribed by the undeserved blessing inherent in the Christian life. Some teachers describe that ideal as the "horizontal" relationship with the cross. Truth is the sometimes harsh expression of the unbending and inarguable dictates within Christ's teachings, which are known as the "vertical" axis on the cross. Examples of truth include that sin must be confessed and called by its name, that receiving forgiveness requires forgiveness of others, and that salvation comes only through Christ.

Every sermon holds a tension between our humility as sinners who need God's grace and the confidence in our salvation as believers. Christians live out their faith with constant appeals to a loving God ("Lord teach us to pray"). Yet most Christians avoid broadcasting their prayers on the sidewalk as the hypocrites and Pharisees did ("vain repetitions"). Most Christians embrace that tension and strive to express their faith thoughtfully. Struggle improves us—on this point, the Bible is quite clear.

In a famous sermon delivered in 1738, Jonathan Edwards asked why the Book of Revelation describes Jesus as "a lion of the tribe of Judah" but he appears a few verses later as a lamb. His quotation at the beginning of this chapter is a lasting monument to the antinomy inherent in Christianity.

Christians who become murderers exemplify self-important fanaticism. Rather than embracing complexity, they default to a black-and-white fantasy world, not unlike a video game in which they are the avenger. These deluded souls skillfully cut and paste scripture, often from the Book of Revelation, to make themselves modern deities (see Charles Manson, David Koresh, and so on). The glorious tension of faith is too much for them.

The trick is to grasp that salt versus light, grace versus truth, and God's sovereignty versus our individual free will aren't opposing half-truths that add up to a whole truth. They are both 100 percent true, all the time—both metal and insulator. That's hard for most of us to get our head around. Fitzgerald was right: antinomy is difficult.

But darn it, why can't our religion be simple? Is that too much to ask? Yes, it is. At some point, we have to embrace that a large part of the value of faith lies in its complexity. It keeps us thinking and humble, which is good—in fact, it is the central premise of Christian life.

CHAPTER EIGHT

A Tool Kit for Centrists

Always phrase a criticism as a question. It leaves the other person a way out—and saves you embarrassment if you are wrong in your premise.

—OVETA CULP HOBBY

If we have learned to acknowledge the value of middle ground— or whatever language we choose to describe the centrist position, the balance point or the golden mean—we need to practice it in our lives. True strength is defined by the weapons we possess but do not deploy.

CIVILITY: MODERATION AS MANNERS

Big cities are associated with lesser manners than small towns because in larger crowds, people assume they're unlikely to see each other again or need to interact on a different subject. In small towns, that assumption fails immediately because you are very likely to see any given person again quite soon, which has a salutatory effect on manners generally. As I discussed in a previous essay, the internet is the ultimate big, anonymous city, and manners suffer.

Good manners are, at their most basic level, civility. Why is that important? Western prosperity has preferred civility not out of weakness or genteel pretense, but because our philosophical heritage, all the way back to Socrates and Cicero, encourages the exchange of ideas. The notion that people can collectively iterate to the best answer is the core premise of representative democracy. Societies without civility, on the other hand, subsist on fear and power. People avoid any display of uncertainty, conflating it with weakness. You can find those nations at the bottom of any list for rising individual income, foreign investment, or in-migration. If you doubt the value of civility, just look at societies that lack it.

Civility is a basic expression of respect for others, but there is also a much more practical effect. Civility is the medium that allows reason and logic to be legitimate currency in any debate, rather than brutish intimidation or defensive behaviors. Jefferson held reason as a supreme collective virtue, regarding emotion as a lesser angel of our nature. He even rearranged his personal Bible in stoic fashion in order to take the miracles and emotion out of the story, preferring to reason his way to Christian belief.

Today's world is more civil and inclusive toward those members of society once marginalized because of their race, religion, or gender. Few would argue that the modern American workplace is less civil than it was even a decade ago, and we are the most productive society on earth as a result.

Beyond manners, civility is better because life is long. The person you can disagree with civilly will be available as an ally on another issue later on. Public servants must eventually master this truism and "do unto others..." Durable leaders know the Golden Rule requires vision beyond the current controversy lest they forfeit the next opportunity before they even know what it is.

For that reason, diplomacy relies on the formalities of civil discourse. The person you disrespect, revile, and insult personally will never take your next argument at face value. People feel the way they feel. Emotion wins over reason if it gets the slightest chance. Fortunately, civility neuters emotion to the extent possible. Accusatory, pointed, invective criticism will do one of two things: make an enemy out of its target or leave us looking foolish.

Thomas Jefferson encapsulated the social benefits of civility in a letter to his grandson Thomas Jefferson Randolph:

> Good humor...is the practice of sacrificing to those whom we meet in society, all the little conveniences and preferences which will gratify them, and deprive us of nothing worth a moment's consideration; it is the giving a pleasing and flattering turn to our expressions, which will conciliate others, and make them pleased with us as well as themselves. How cheap a price for the goodwill of another!

MIDDLE PERFECT

If you need a brilliant example of balance, the Declaration of Independence is the poster child for applied antimony. Penned by Jefferson, but revised by committee, it is our seminal document, our rallying cry as a great nation-in-waiting. No place, then, for balance, surely; it is, by its terms, an act of harshest defiance meant to incite action on the part of those who read it. It is perhaps the last place you might look for the middle, but look anyway.

In that Declaration, Jefferson claims that "all men...are endowed by their Creator with certain unalienable Rights," making our cause transcendent and spiritual at its core. He eloquently and confidently states that among those rights "are Life, Liberty and the pursuit of Happiness." The former is explicitly spiritual, while the latter is an entirely secular humanist concept. In his Pulitzer Prize–winning book *The Swerve*, Stephen Greenblatt traces that phrase word for word back to the Roman poet and philosopher Lucretius.

Lucretius established the tenets of Epicureanism, promoting the idea of pleasure during one's earthly lifetime, as opposed to Godly pleasure reserved for the afterlife. As you can suppose, Epicureans were the scourge of the religious authorities in the fifteenth century. The masterpiece of Jefferson's prose is that neither spiritualism nor secular humanism capitulates to the other—it is boldly both, in a graceful alloy of ideas.

The elegance of the Declaration of Independence, meant not just for aspiring Americans of its time but for a global audience and the larger sweep of history, is now self-evident. It is a perfect alloy.

COLLECTIVE SECURITY VERSUS INDIVIDUAL LIBERTY

America was created to resolve the security-versus-liberty question on the side of liberty to the greatest extent possible. Many domestic political debates turn on the question of where to draw that line. Perfect liberty, where everyone is free to drive on whichever side of the road they see fit, would create a dangerous state of chaos. Perfect security, on the other hand, where Chinese-style obedience is the only option, would stifle individualism and produce an oppressive society. Notice that, in this respect, communism—in which security nominally preserves Marx's "dictatorship of the proletariat"—is indistinguishable in practice from fascism, in which security is nominally for the benefit of the state. Do not lose the logical thread here: *any ideology is a farce when corrupt people hold the power to apply it.*

Just as day follows night, despots of any variety will use the straw man of collective security to repress individual liberties. The ruling classes will seek to perpetuate their power in any system; it's just easier to do so in some systems than in others. Look no further than any recent newspaper to find a corrupt potentate warning of "dangerous foreign agents," creating a convenient diversion from their own incompetence or corruption.

A leader who can scare you or convince you to be fearful of others can and will control you. Thus, President John F. Kennedy was right: fear itself is the enemy. It will steal your liberty if you let it. We all trade liberty for security in large and small ways each day, but volition in each circumstance—the consent of the governed—is the American way in which we strike the proper balance.

CHAPTER NINE

Applying the Tool Kit: Rules for Radical Centrists

Neither rash nor hesitant—nor bewildered or at a loss...not obsequious—but be not aggressive or paranoid either.

—MARCUS AURELIUS

The best practical way to practice constructive moderation is to cultivate a willingness to doubt your own mind. Our worldview is the product of our experiences and observations. As we have seen, once installed, our opinions crystallize naturally into harder and harder conclusions. Pride and arrogance creep in. To borrow from David Brooks, we must create "firebreaks of decorum" to soften our outward certainty. *Don't Believe Everything You Think* is the title of a recent popular book that reminds us the easiest person to fool is always yourself.

Be curious. I had a football coach who used to say, "If you're green, you are growing; if you are ripe, you're rotting." So be green. We should laugh at ourselves. Accept contradiction. Embrace the antinomy around us. Consider that there are insane people who agree with us and sane people who disagree.

The best-defined framework or practical methodology I have seen to apply antinomy is from the late Rushworth Kidder, former chief executive of the Institute for Global Ethics. In his book *How Good People Make Tough Choices*, Kidder outlines the "right versus right" decision paradigm, then places a logical frame around any difficult choice. Those decisions exist in contrast to "right versus wrong" decisions, which are not logical dilemmas at all, but are better thought of as temptations. Reason is seldom involved in those choices; one of the seven deadly sins almost always is.

"Right versus right" choices have high-quality arguments on both sides yet require a decision. These are instances when judgment is unavoidable and inclusion has to be part of the equation. Respect for minority opinion is an acceptable form of balance, even if the decision is not to their liking. Why else would minority opinions of the Supreme Court even get published?

Kidder creates a framework of antinomies that encapsulate the vast majority of legitimate dilemmas in order to accomplish that balance:

- **Justice versus mercy** comes into play when fairness, justice, and policy conflict with compassion and empathy.
- **Short-term versus long-term** decisions arise when immediate needs and desires run counter to future goals or prospects.
- **Individual versus community** dilemmas can be restated as

us versus them, self versus others, or *the smaller group versus the larger group.*

- **Truth versus loyalty** choices involve candor or integrity on one side and commitment or responsibility on the other.

Kidder lays out examples of real-world dilemmas and works through them methodically, applying one or more of his frameworks to the fact pattern of each.

As I wrote much of this book, during the long tail of the coronavirus pandemic, leaders around the world struggled with a framework for decisions as they faced difficult "right versus right" choices. Most saw the preservation of life in tension with the preservation of livelihood and commerce. That dilemma is not simple to navigate. If they didn't understand this basic rule of leadership before, they do now: *it's not a decision if everyone agrees with it.*

CHAPTER TEN

Action Items
for Centrists

*But so long as men are not trained to withhold judgement in the
absence of evidence, they will be led astray by cocksure prophets,
and it is likely that their leaders will be either ignorant fanatics
or dishonest charlatans. To be sure uncertainty is difficult, but
so are most of the other virtues.*

—BERTRAND RUSSELL, *UNPOPULAR ESSAYS*

I promised that we would eventually come back to Martin
Luther King Jr.'s quote about "the silence of our friends" and
consider it in a new light. This is that moment where the prism
of his words refract, not as criticism of friends who fail to support you but of friends who fail to correct us. Let uncertainty
be difficult; it will make us less susceptible to ignorant fanatics
or dishonest charlatans peddling simple answers.

POLICING OUR PEOPLE

Finally, a difficult action item: the first step toward bolstering the middle requires acknowledging what we can affect and what we cannot. We cannot affect those on the "other side." We can outspend them, we can outshout them, we can win an election— but we can't change them. Remember what we've learned about the human mind: successful persuasion doesn't come through frontal assault. Carl Jung was right in noting people don't have ideas; ideas have people. Love and the behaviors that come with it are our only chance. Empathy arises from acknowledging that in some respects, you are as flawed as your opponent on the issue of the moment.

The second step contains better news: we *can* affect our own people, because we are inside their tribe, in their foxhole, on their side. If our social media presence involves zealously satirizing the wacky people on the left or the wacky people on the right but is silent when our own tribe crosses a line, there is a word for us. That word is coward. We are scared to be ostracized by our own circle of belief, so we hide behind specious arguments: "the popular media does plenty of that so I don't have to," or "I'm just defending freedom," or "I'm just sticking it to the man."

Seneca, the stoic philosopher and statesman, declared that "excellence withers without an adversary." This is the secular version of the biblical passage "Iron sharpens iron." The point is that conflict is not evil but rather necessary, most especially among erstwhile allies.

People who speak up when their friends fool themselves are judged well by history. Bari Weiss is the most prominent person on the left to have defied her tribe. She had achieved liberal nirvana as the editor of the *New York Times* editorial page but famously resigned from her dream job when wokeness became intellectually unsustainable. Liz Cheney is the most prominent person on the right who has defied her tribe. When she called January 6 an insurrection, she was quite literally evicted from her party's leadership and beaten badly by a primary opponent who held the line for election and insurrection deniers. Both Weiss and Cheney have paid a career price and been called traitors. They no longer have a base, but they have something more valuable: a real set of standards that requires rebellion when their "side" loses its moorings.

How do we distinguish constructive friction from the destructive variety?

Look back at the verb *sharpen*. Useful friction is the kind that requires mutual sacrifice. If both sides lose some metal at the edges, the blade benefits. If one party countenances no regret, accepts no compromise, allows no admission of error, and tolerates no lost metal, that is evidence of destructive friction because it's not improving the result.

If Islam has a problem, it won't be Christians who fix it. If Christianity has a problem, it won't be Muslims who fix it. If certain Democrats lose their social and economic moorings, other Democrats have an obligation to police their party. If certain Republicans fall down the rabbit hole of violence in the name of patriotism, other Republicans need to stand for their core beliefs peacefully. Lasting change comes from the inside.

The middle can emerge only when the faithful question themselves. Two sides only reconcile if self-reflective members of

their own parties hold the zealots, the ideologues, and the dogmatists to some standard of consistency, decency, and factual
accuracy. If we are on a "fighting side" rather than seeking truth
and peaceful coexistence, not only are we not part of the solution; we are absolutely part of the problem.

Author's Postscript

I'll wind up with a personal story. In June 1987, I was a baby lawyer dispatched to supervise document production in a huge lawsuit at Comanche Peak, a nuclear plant under construction near Glen Rose, Texas. It was summertime hot on the shadeless caliche jobsite. When I complained to my mother about my state of affairs, she suggested that I should go see an old colleague of hers, John Graves, who lived nearby. She knew I loved Graves's books, especially *Goodbye to a River*. Nonetheless, just dropping in on this icon of Texas letters seemed audacious, and I told my mother so. She said, "Nonsense. He'd love to see you. I'll call and set it up." So she did just that, and I'm so grateful I went.

We spent a few hours on his unfinished porch, scattered about with limestone pieces, empty Copenhagen tins, bags of Sakrete mortar, and an old mixing machine. He was building his own house in no particular hurry. His contracting skills were pretty average, but the man's verbal brilliance was on full display. The words that spilled casually from his mouth were like little diamonds hitting the floor. As cliché as it sounds, I was actually transfixed in the presence of such foundational, pithy wisdom and worried that if I ran to my truck to get something to write on, somehow the spell would break. So I concentrated hard to memorize the best of his gems. Driving away, I stopped at the end of his driveway to scribble furiously all I could remember on whatever paper I had.

One of those diamonds was this: he looked at me casually after relating an observation about modernism—not a complaint but an observation—and said, "Paul, a man like me shouldn't enjoy a world like this, but I do." I think of that as glorious tension applied. Happiness is a decision, but one that requires balance, compromise, discipline, forgiveness, mystery, and wisdom. Graves, an untroubled truth seeker, had just defined the practical virtue of avoiding torment by ideology or doctrine. Mental health and the capacity for kindness and love—yes, love—are improved by humility that acknowledges shades of gray in the universe. The humility to respect fine people who think differently, because we are all shaped by life's unique experiences.

The dry optimism of Graves's remark has often been a sentinel for me over the years. You have to enjoy the times you live in, however tragic or absurd, because the cynical alternative is an insult to the marvel of life itself. Apart from that personal conversation, my favorite passage from Graves's published work is one in *Hard Scrabble* about his notion of "old reality":

> You see it and it sees you. Old reality survives, blinking at you there, lizard-eyed. Survives and will prevail.

> That is perhaps enough to know. Yes.

His notion of old reality has a "dust to dust" quality that appeals in its constancy. It is patient and tied to the wisdom of the land itself. That the present belongs to eternity is perhaps the most antimonious notion of all. I took a long while to find comfort in my own notion of old reality, but now I know the world self-corrects.

We need patience, but the middle ultimately wins. And it should.

At what cost it wins depends on whether each of us treats the sacrament of consensus as an active pursuit. The middle isn't about trying to please everyone. In fact, it pleases no one completely. Glorious tension creates its own reward. The strength of the old reality within our centrist alloy comes not from momentary victories, but from the stubborn substrate of reason—the delicate equilibrium of form, function, grace, truth, freedom, security, and all the other antinomies we have examined.

Acknowledgments

I would like to thank the many people who were unaware they were test audiences for much of this messaging—dinner partners, family members, coworkers, and friends. For much of that exercise I wasn't aware that this was a book either. But the iterative method certainly helped animate what is on its face, a contradiction: making the middle an exciting idea. I don't think it's a page-turner by any measure, but if it is at least a coherent statement, that is because people like Peter Kiernan, Ryan Holiday, Walker Hobby, Dan Goodgame, and Darren Walker read early drafts and were kind but candid in their feedback. Thank you also to the team at Scribe Media for being the citation police, the timekeepers, and the encouragers as this project came together.

Thank you finally to the late Dan Jenkins, who penned silly, immortal words to the ballad of the moderate in his bestseller *Semi-Tough.*

The musical character was Elroy Blunt, and the song was titled "Nuthin Much to Want."

Here is the refrain:

I could halfway fall in love,

For part of a lonely night

With a semi pretty woman in my arms

Before anyone has a fit of political correctness, remember that David Halberstam gave the book a rousing recommendation in the *New York Times* in 1972. A quote from that review:

> Dan Jenkins of Sports Illustrated has written a book that is about sports, but not about sports, and it is a very funny book. A marvelous book. I loved it. I read it aloud to my wife, who does not like football one bit, and she loved it. It is outrageous; it mocks contemporary American mores; it mocks Madison Avenue; it mocks racial attitudes; it mocks writers like me; and it even mocks sportswriters for Sports Illustrated like Dan Jenkins.

So let's skip the righteous umbrage and laugh instead. Let's mock ourselves and know that keeps us centered, healthy, and loving.

Cheers,

Paul Hobby

Works Referenced

Ashish. "What Is Hybrid Vigor?" ScienceABC. Last updated July 8, 2022. https://www.scienceabc.com/nature/what-is-hybrid-vigor-definition-examples-and-a-brief-explanation.html.

Avidon, Claire. "In Our 'Crisis of Contempt,' How Can Christians Disagree with Others—Gracefully?" Denison Forum. February 20, 2020. https://www.denisonforum.org/columns/contributor-article/in-our-crisis-of-contempt-how-can-christians-disagree-with-others-gracefully/.

Brooks, Arthur C. "America's Crisis of Contempt." Opinion, *Washington Post*, February 7, 2020. https://www.washingtonpost.com/opinions/2020/02/07/arthur-brooks-national-prayer-breakfast-speech/?arc404=true&itid=lk_interstitial_manual_8.

Brooks, David. *The Road to Character*. New York: Random House, 2015.

Carleton, Don. *The Governor and the Colonel: A Dual Biography of William P. Hobby and Oveta Culp Hobby*. Austin: Briscoe Center for American History, 2021.

Dostoevsky, Fyodor. *The Brothers Karamazov: A Novel in Four Parts with Epilogue*. Translated by Richard Paver and Larissa Volokhonsky. New York: Farrar, Straus and Giroux, 1990.

Draper, Robert. "Did America Misjudge Bernie Sanders? Or Did He Misjudge America?" *New York Times Magazine,* March 16, 2020. https://www.nytimes.com/2020/03/16/magazine/bernie-sanders-campaign.html.

"Dunning-Kruger Effect." *Psychology Today,* accessed January 30, 2023. https://www.psychologytoday.com/us/basics/dunning-kruger-effect.

"Extract from Thomas Jefferson to Charles Yancey." Jefferson Quotes & Family. Accessed January 30, 2023. https://tjrs.monticello.org/letter/327.

Flanagan, Caitlin. "Why the Left Is So Afraid of Jordan Peterson." *The Atlantic,* August 9, 2018. https://www.theatlantic.com/ideas/archive/2018/08/why-the-left-is-so-afraid-of-jordan-peterson/567110/.

"From Thomas Jefferson to John Taylor, 4 June 1798." Founders Online. Accessed January 30, 2023. https://founders.archives.gov/documents/Jefferson/01-30-02-0280.

"From Thomas Jefferson to Thomas Jefferson Randolph, 24 November 1808." Founders Online. Accessed January 30, 2023. https://founders.archives.gov/documents/Jefferson/99-01-02-9151.

Gawdat, Mo. *Solve for Happy: Engineer Your Path to Joy.* New York: North Star Way, 2017.

Gladwell, Malcolm. *David and Goliath: Underdogs, Misfits, and the Art of Battling Giants.* New York: Little, Brown and Company, 2013.

Graves, John. *Hard Scrabble: Observations on a Patch of Land.* New York: Knopf, 1974.

Greenblatt, Stephen. *The Swerve: How the World Became Modern.* New York: W. W. Norton & Company, 2011.

Hobby, Oveta Culp. "It Can Happen Here." Rice Digital Scholarship Archive. Accessed January 30, 2023. https://scholarship.rice.edu/handle/1911/78571.

Horwitz, Jeff, and Deepa Seetharaman. "Facebook Executives Shut Down Efforts to Make the Site Less Divisive." *Wall Street Journal*, May 26, 2020. https://www.wsj.com/articles/facebook-knows-it-encourages-division-top-executives-nixed-solutions-11590507499.

Isaacson, Walter. *Benjamin Franklin: An American Life*. New York: Simon & Schuster Paperbacks, 2004.

Kidder, Rushworth M. *How Good People Make Tough Choices: Resolving the Dilemmas of Ethical Living*. New York: William Morrow, 1995.

Klein, Ezra. *Why We're Polarized*. New York: Avid Reader Press, 2020.

Meacham, Jon. *The Hope of Glory: Reflections on the Last Words of Jesus from the Cross*. New York: Convergent Books, 2020.

Morton, Frederic. *Thunder at Twilight: Vienna 1913–1914*. Boston: Da Capo Press, 2014.

Rosling, Hans, Ola Rosling, and Anna Rosling Rönnlund. *Factfulness: Ten Reasons We're Wrong about the World—and Why Things Are Better Than You Think*. New York: Flatiron Books, 2018.

Russell, Bertrand. *Unpopular Essays*. New York: Routledge, 2009.

Will, George F. *The Conservative Sensibility*. New York: Hachette Books, 2019.

"Winston Churchill versus Joseph Chamberlain." Lincoln & Churchill, Lehrman Institute. Accessed January 30, 2023. https://lincolnandchurchill.org/896-2/.

Yeats, William Butler. "The Second Coming." Poetry Foundation. Accessed January 30, 2023. https://www.poetryfoundation.org/poems/43290/the-second-coming.